# World Languages

# FRENCH

## For Kids

Written & Illustrated
By Sachiko Otohata

We have dedicated considerable time and effort to ensure the accuracy and cultural sensitivity of our content. However, if you find any errors or have suggestions, please feel free to contact us at factorysachi.com. Your input is crucial for us to refine and improve our offerings for young learners.

If you enjoyed this book, please consider leaving a review online. As an independent publisher, every review helps more parents and children discover and learn about this book.

factorysachi.com
factorysachi (Instagram/Facebook/Pinterest)

Don't forget to check out the rest of the World Languages series.

Fun and educational companion books for coloring, activities, drawing, and taking notes!

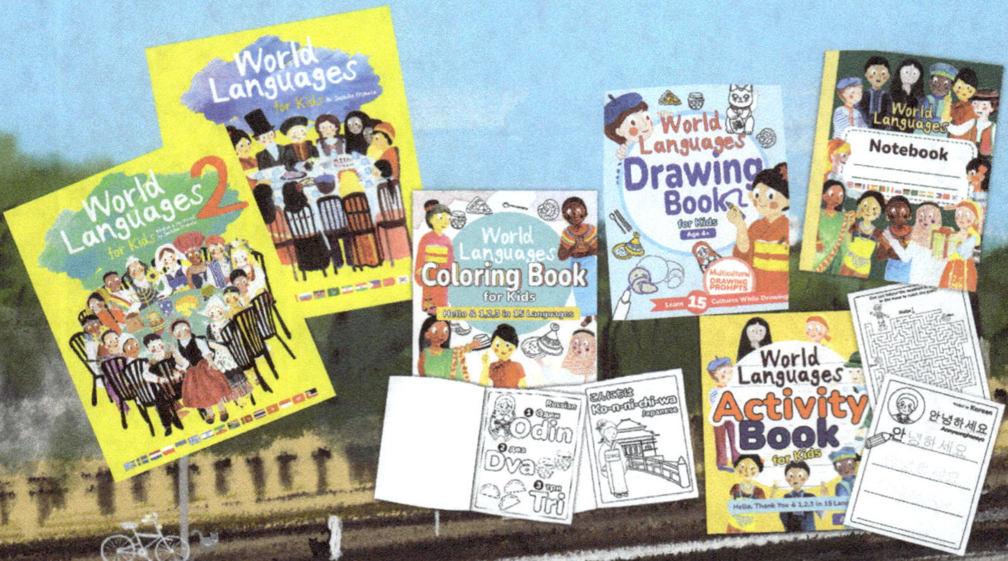

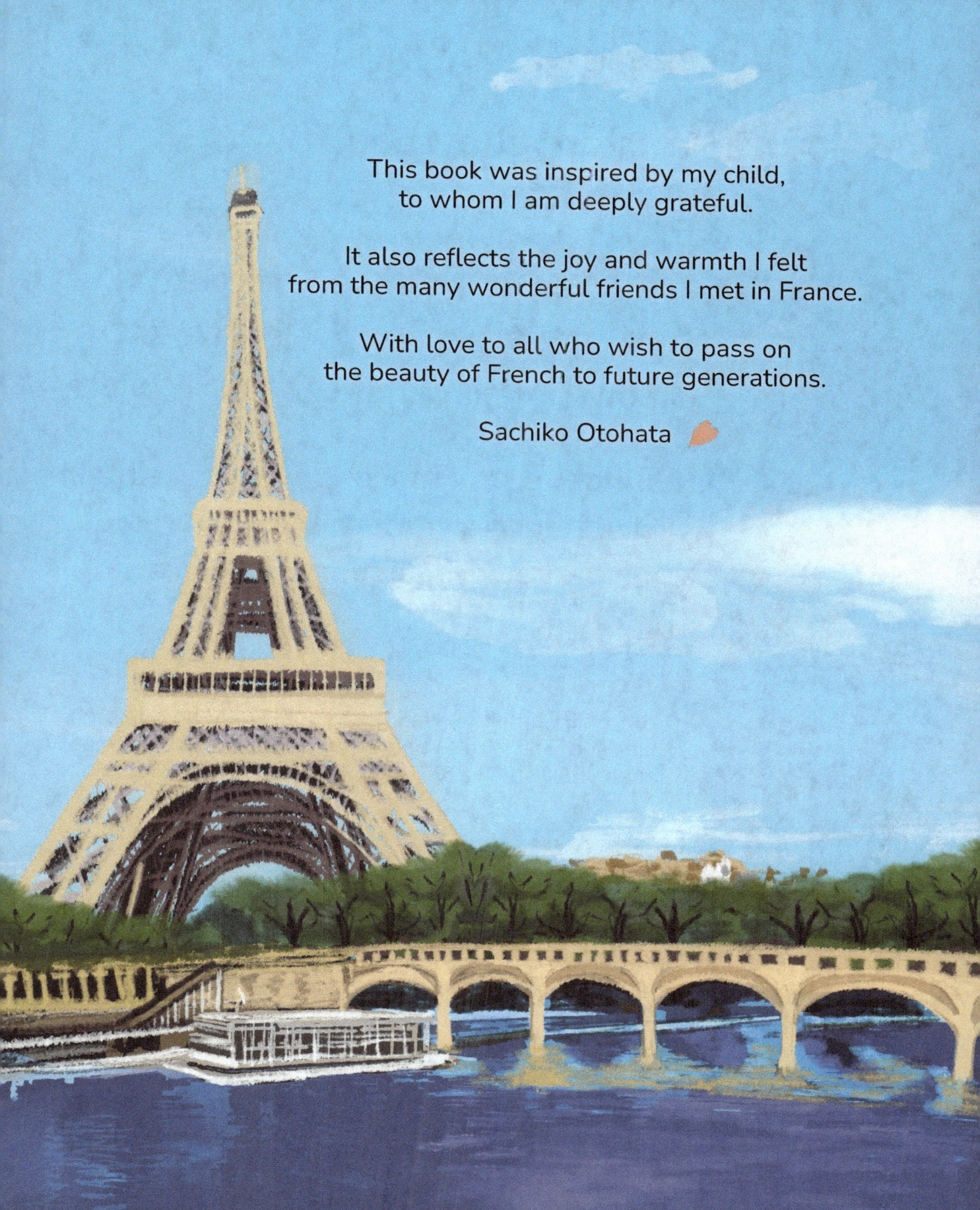

This book was inspired by my child,
to whom I am deeply grateful.

It also reflects the joy and warmth I felt
from the many wonderful friends I met in France.

With love to all who wish to pass on
the beauty of French to future generations.

Sachiko Otohata

# Hello! My name is Léon.

## Bonjour ! Je m'appelle Léon.

bohn-JOOR ! juh mah-PELL lay-OHN

I live in France, a country full of delicious food, lovely art, and magical places to explore!

J'habite en France, un pays plein de plats délicieux, de belles œuvres d'art et de lieux magiques à explorer !

jah-BEET ahn FRAHNSS, uhn peh-EE plehn duh plah day-lee-SYEW, duh bell ZUHV ruh dahr ay duh lyeu mah-JEEK ah eks-ploh-RAY !

Atlantic Ocean

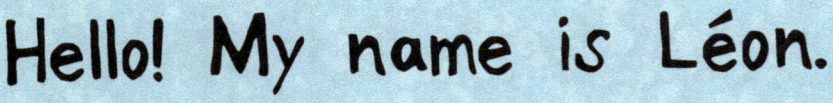

One of the most beautiful things in my world is the French language.

L'une des plus belles choses dans mon monde, c'est la langue française.

luhn day ploo BEL shohz dahn mohn MOHND, seh lah lahn-g frahn-SEZ

Like a little key, each new word you learn opens a new door to understanding people and places.

Comme une petite clé, chaque nouveau mot que tu apprends ouvre une porte vers la compréhension des gens et des lieux.

kohm uhn puh-TEET clay, shak noo-VOH moh kuh tew ah-PRAHN oovr uhn PORT vehr lah kohm-prohn-SYOHN day jahn ay dayz LYUH

# Would you like to discover some of my favorite French words?

## Tu veux découvrir mes mots français préférés ?

tew vuh day-koo-VREER meh moh frahn-SEH pray-fay-RAY

# How to Use This Book:

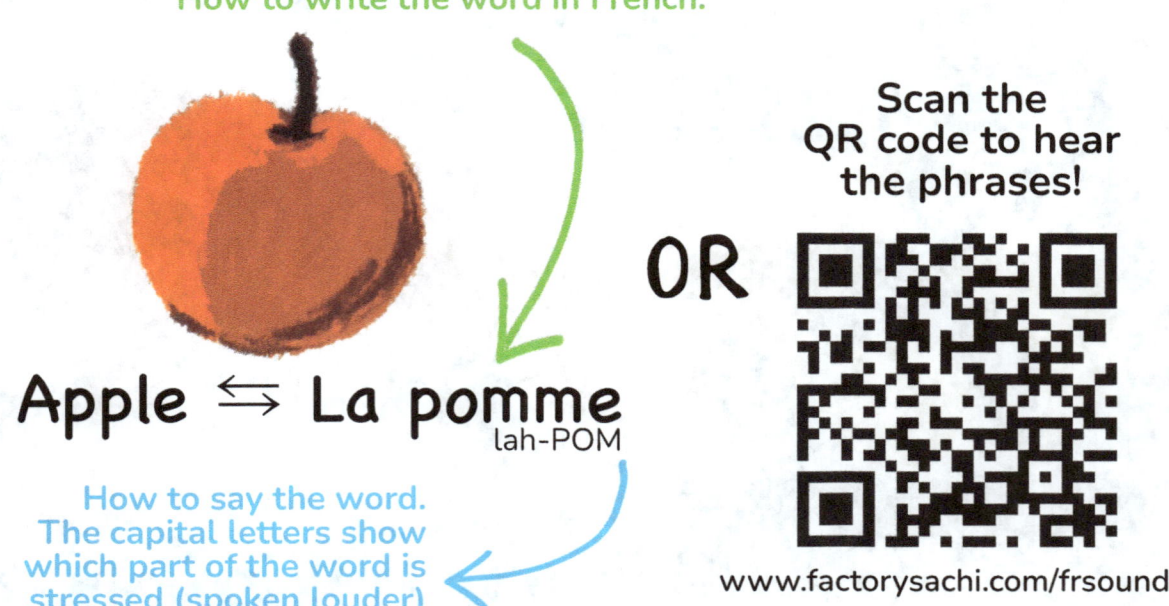

How to write the word in French.

Scan the QR code to hear the phrases!

Apple ⇆ La pomme
lah-POM

OR

How to say the word. The capital letters show which part of the word is stressed (spoken louder)

www.factorysachi.com/frsound

Everyone speaks a little differently! The pronunciation shown in this book is just a helpful guide — you might hear small differences depending on who is speaking.

Good night ⇆ **Bonne nuit**
**bohn NWEE**

Thank you ⇆ **Merci**
**mehr-SEE**

Sorry ⇆ **Désolé**
**day-zo-LAY**

Please ⇆ **S'il vous plaît /
S'il te plaît**
**seel voo PLEH / seel tuh PLEH**

Excuse me ⇆ **Excusez-moi / Excuse-moi**
**ex-KYOO-zay mwah / ex-KYOOZ mwah**

I love you ⇆ **Je t'aime**
**juh TEM**

Hello ⇆ **Bonjour**
**bohn-JOOR**

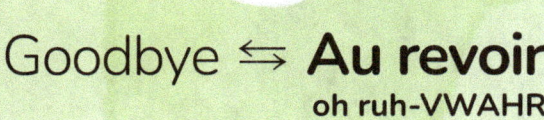

Goodbye ⇆ **Au revoir**
**oh ruh-VWAHR**

Everyday Phrases ⇆ **Les expressions du quotidien**
**lay ex-preh-SYOHN dew koh-tee-DYAN**

Younger brother
⇆ **Le petit frère**
luh puh-TEE FRAIR

Younger sister
⇆ **La petite sœur**
lah puh-TEET SIR

Older sister
⇆ **La grande sœur**
lah grahnd SIR

Older brother
⇆ **Le grand frère**
luh grahn FRAIR

Aunt ⇆ **La tante**
lah TAHNT

Uncle ⇆ **L'oncle**
LONG-kluh

Baby ⇆ **Le bébé**
luh bay-BAY

Cousin
⇆ **Le cousin / La cousine**
luh koo-ZAN / lah koo-ZEEN

Grandmother ⇆ **La grand-mère**
lah grahn-MAIR

Grandfather ⇆ **Le grand-père**
luh grahn-PAIR

Father ⇆ **Le père**
luh PAIR

Mother ⇆ **La mère**
lah MAIR

**Who do you live with?**
⇆ **Avec qui est-ce que tu habites ?**
ah-VEK kee ess kuh tew ah-BEET

Pet ⇆ **Un animal**
ahn ah-nee-MAL

Family ⇆ **La famille**
lah fah-MEE

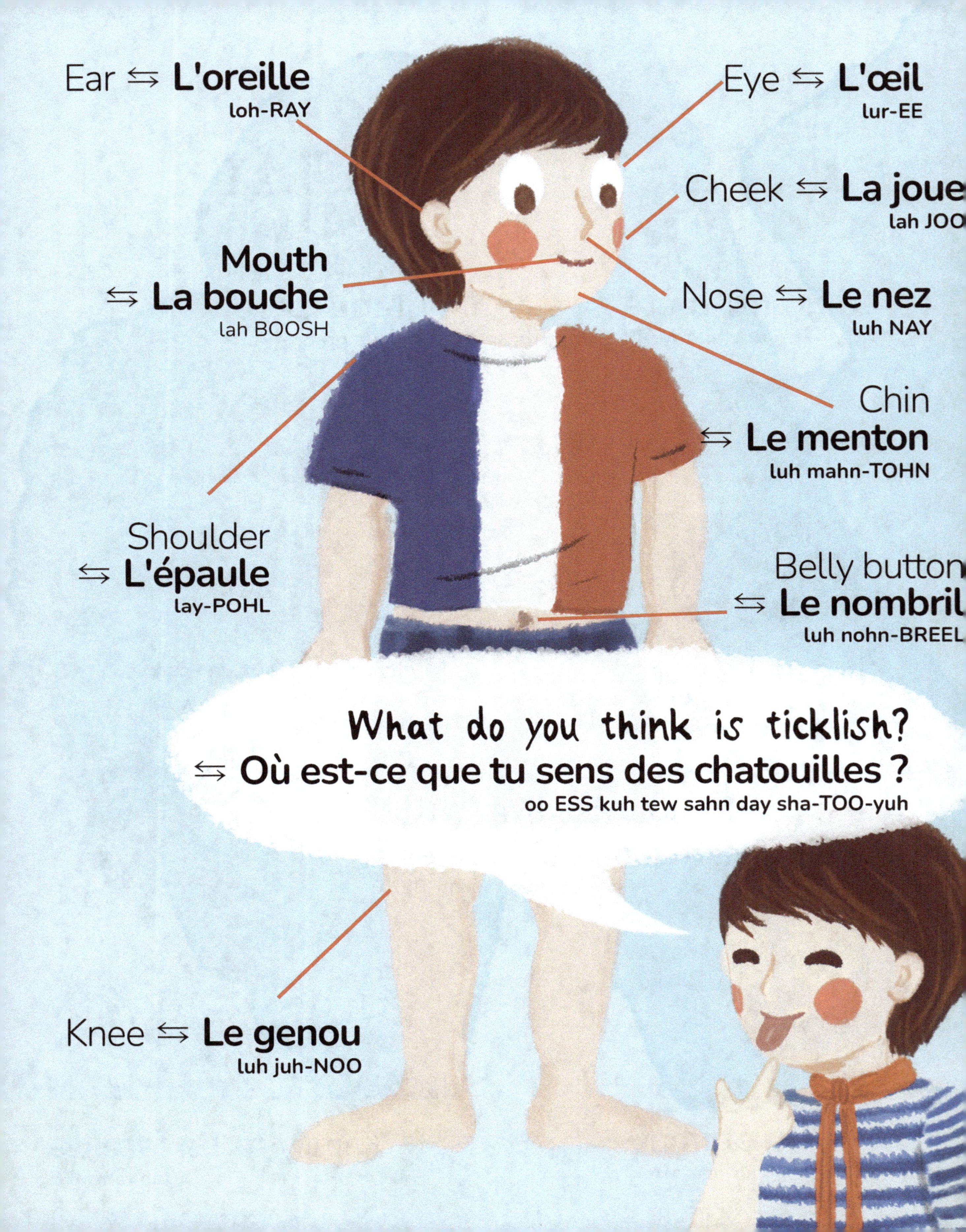

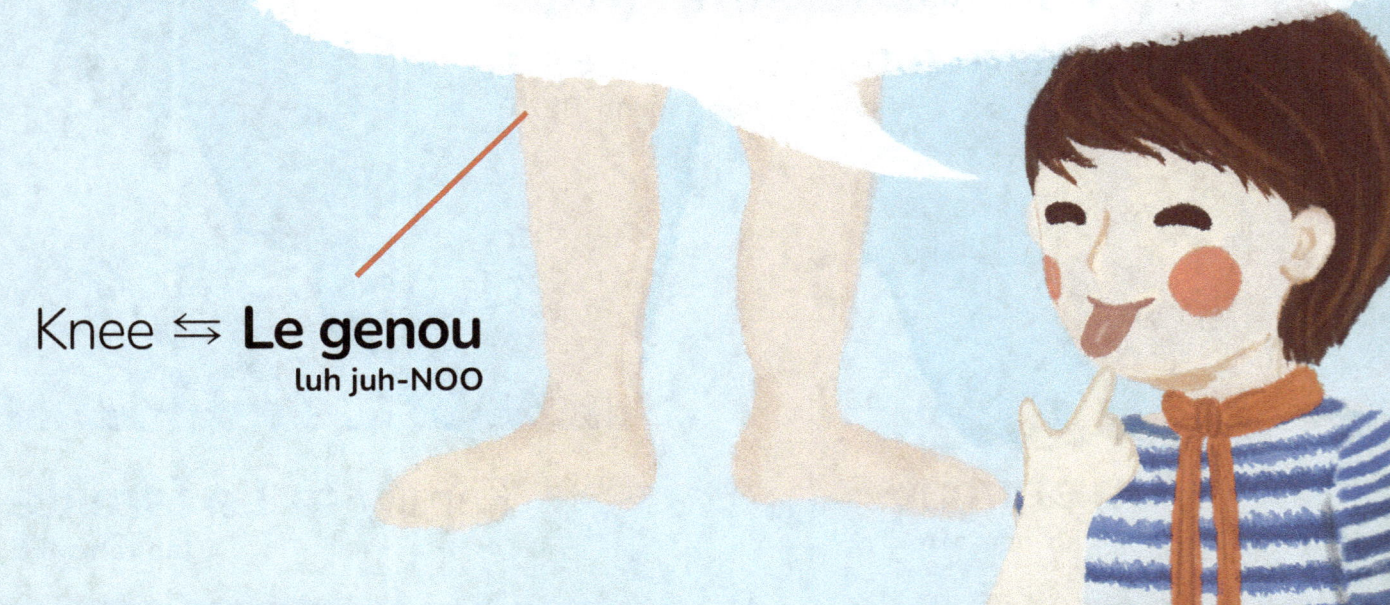

Ear ⇆ **L'oreille**
loh-RAY

Eye ⇆ **L'œil**
lur-EE

Cheek ⇆ **La joue**
lah JOO

**Mouth**
⇆ **La bouche**
lah BOOSH

Nose ⇆ **Le nez**
luh NAY

Chin
⇆ **Le menton**
luh mahn-TOHN

Shoulder
⇆ **L'épaule**
lay-POHL

Belly button
⇆ **Le nombril**
luh nohn-BREEL

**What do you think is ticklish?**
⇆ **Où est-ce que tu sens des chatouilles ?**
oo ESS kuh tew sahn day sha-TOO-yuh

Knee ⇆ **Le genou**
luh juh-NOO

Hair ⇆ **Les cheveux**
lay shuh-VUH

Head ⇆ **La tête**
lah TET

Neck ⇆ **Le cou**
luh KOO

Armpit ⇆ **L'aisselle**
lay-SELL

Elbow ⇆ **Le coude**
luh KOOD

Hand ⇆ **La main**
lah MAN

Finger ⇆ **Le doigt**
luh DWA

Bum ⇆ **Les fesses**
lay FESS

Leg ⇆ **La jambe**
lah JAHMB

Toe ⇆ **L'orteil**
lor-TAY

Body ⇆ **Le corps**
luh KOR

Shirt ⇆ **La chemise**
lah shuh-MEEZ

Pajamas ⇆ **Le pyjama**
luh pee-ja-MAH

Dress ⇆ **La robe**
lah ROB

Skirt ⇆ **La jupe**
lah JOOP

Socks ⇆ **Les chaussettes**
lay show-SET

Shoes ⇆ **Les chaussures**
lay show-SOOR

Pants ⇆ **Le pantalon**
luh pahn-tah-LOHN

Hat ⇆ **Le chapeau**
luh sha-POH

T-shirt ⇆ **Le T-shirt**
**luh tee-SHURT**

Bag ⇆ **Le sac**
**luh SAK**

Underwear ⇆ **Les sous-vêtements**
**lay soo-vet-MOHN**

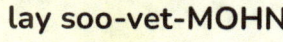

Scarf ⇆ **L'écharpe**
**lay-SHARP**

Gloves ⇆ **Les gants**
**lay GAHN**

**What are you wearing?**
⇆ **Qu'est-ce que tu portes ?**
**kes kuh tew PORT**

Glasses ⇆ **Les lunettes**
**lay loo-NET**

Clothes ⇆ **Les vêtements**
**lay vet-MOHN**

Draw ⇆ **Dessiner**
day-see-NAY

Sing ⇆ **Chanter**
shahn-TAY

Play ⇆ **Jouer**
joo-AY

Cook ⇆ **Cuisiner**
kwee-zee-NAY

Read ⇆ **Lire**
LEE-ruh

Eat ⇆ **Manger**
mahn-JAY

Sleep ⇆ **Dormir**
dor-MEER

Drink ⇆ **Boire**
BWAHR

What do you like to do?
⇆ Qu'est-ce que tu aimes faire ?
kes kuh tew EM fair

Wash ⇆ **Laver**
lah-VAY

Things to do ⇆ **Les actions**
lay zak-SYOHN

Bananas ⇆ **La banane**
lah bah-NAHN

Strawberries ⇆ **Les fraises**
lay FREHZ

Apple ⇆ **La pomme**
lah POM

Corn ⇆ **Le maïs**
luh mah-EES

Grapes ⇆ **Les raisins**
lay ray-ZAN

Carrot ⇆ **La carotte**
lah kah-ROHT

Mushrooms ⇆ **Les champignons**
lay shahm-pee-NYOHN

Tomato ⇆ **La tomate**
lah toh-MAHT

Onion ⇆ **L'oignon**
loh-NYON

Cheese ⇆ **Le fromage**
luh froh-MAHJ

Potato ⇆ **La pomme de terre**
lah pom duh TAIR

Cucumber ⇆ **Le concombre**
luh kohn-KOHM-bruh

Yogurt ⇆ **Le yaourt**
luh yah-OORT

Milk ⇆ **Le lait**
luh LAY

Candies ⇆ **Les bonbons**
lay bon-BOHN

Bread ⇆ **Le pain**
luh PAN

**What do you think is yummy?**
⇆ **Qu'est-ce que tu trouves délicieux ?**
kes kuh tew troov day-lee-SYEUH

Fish ⇆ **Le poisson**
luh pwah-SOHN

Egg ⇆ **L'œuf**
LUHF

Food ⇆ **La nourriture**
lah noo-ree-TOOR

Window ⇆ **La fenêtre**
lah fuh-NEHT-ruh

Mirror ⇆ **Le miroir**
luh meer-WAHR

Curtain ⇆ **Le rideau**
luh ree-DOH

Plant ⇆ **La plante**
lah PLANT

Pillow ⇆ **L'oreille**
lor-AY-ye

Bed ⇆ **Le lit**
luh LEE

Blanket ⇆ **La couverture**
lah koo-vehr-TEWR

Wall ⇆ **Le mur**
luh MYUR

Clock ⇆ **L'horloge**
lor-LOHJ

Door ⇆ **La porte**
lah PORT

Chair ⇆ **La chaise**
lah SHEZ

Lamp ⇆ **La lampe**
lah LAHMP

Desk ⇆ **Le bureau**
luh byu-ROH

**What's in your room?**
⇆ **Qu'est-ce qu'il y a dans ta chambre?**
kes keel yah dahn tah SHAHM-bruh

Room ⇆ **La chambre**
lah SHAHM-bruh

Cow ⇆ **La vache**
lah VASH

Pig ⇆ **Le cochon**
luh koh-SHOHN

Squirrel ⇆ **L'écureuil**
lay-kyur-AY

Chicken ⇆ **La poule**
lah POOL

Mouse ⇆ **La souris**
lah SOO-ree

Dog ⇆ **Le chien**
luh SHYAHN

Rabbit ⇆ **Le lapin**
luh lah-PAHN

Bird ⇆ **L'oiseau**
luh-wah-ZOH

Horse ⇆ **Le cheval**
luh shuh-VAL

Fox ⇆ **Le renard**
luh ruh-NAR

Sheep ⇆ **Le mouton**
luh moo-TOHN

Cat ⇆ **Le chat**
luh SHAH

What's your favorite animal?
⇆ **Quel est ton animal préféré ?**
kel eh ton ah-nee-MAL pray-fay-RAY

Duck ⇆ **Le canard**
luh kah-NAR

Animals ⇆ **Les animaux**
lay zah-nee-MOH

Moon ⇆ **La lune**
lah LOON

Star ⇆ **L'étoile**
lay-TWAHL

Mountain ⇆ **La montagne**
lah mohn-TAN-ye

Lake ⇆ **Le lac**
luh LAK

Tree ⇆ **L'arbre**
LAR-bruh

River ⇆ **La rivière**
lah ree-VYEHR

Rock ⇆ **La roche**
lah ROSH

Sun ⇆ **Le soleil**
luh soh-LAY

Sky ⇆ **Le ciel**
luh SYEL

Ocean ⇆ **L'océan**
loh-say-AHN

**What do you think is beautiful?**
⇆
**Qu'est-ce que tu trouves beau ?**
kes kuh tew troov BOH

Flower ⇆ **La fleur**
lah FLUR

Nature ⇆ **La nature**
lah nah-TOOR

Rainy ⇆ **Pluvieux**
ploo-VYUH

Cloudy ⇆ **Nuageux**
nwah-JUR

Sunny ⇆ **Ensoleillé**
ahn-soh-LAY-yeh

Windy ⇆ **Venteux**
vahn-TUH

Snowy ⇆ **Neigeux**
neh-JUR

Rainbow ⇆ **L'arc-en-ciel**
lahr-k-ahn-SYEL

Lightning ⇆ **L'éclair**
lay-KLAIR

Spring ⇆ **Le printemps**
**luh pran-TAHN**

Summer ⇆ **L'été**
**lay-TAY**

Fall ⇆ **L'automne**
**loh-TUHN**

Winter ⇆ **L'hiver**
**lee-VEHR**

**What's the weather like today?**
⇆ **Quel temps fait-il aujourd'hui ?**
**kel ton feh-TEEL oh-joor-DWEE**

Seasons & Weather ⇆ **Les saisons et le temps**
**lay seh-ZOHN ay luh TAHN**

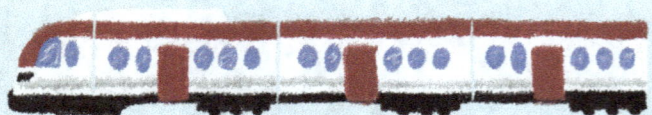

Train ⇆ **Le train**
**luh TRAN**

Car ⇆ **La voiture**
**lah vwah-TOOR**

Bicycle ⇆ **Le vélo**
**luh vay-LOH**

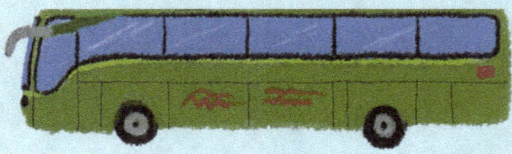

Bus ⇆ **Le bus**
**luh BUS**

Airplane ⇆ **L'avion**
**lah-vyohn**

Police car ⇆ **La voiture de police**
**lah vwah-TOOR duh poh-LEE**

Fire truck ⇆ **Le camion de pompiers**
**luh kah-myohn duh pom-PYAY**

Truck ⇆ **Le camion**
**luh kah-MYON**

Motorcycle ⇆ **La moto**
**lah moh-TOH**

Helicopter ⇆ **L'hélicoptère**
**lay-lee-kop-TAIR**

Ambulance ⇆ **L'ambulance**
**lahm-byu-LAHNS**

**What would you like to ride?**
⇆ **Qu'est-ce que tu veux prendre ?**
**kes kuh tew vuh PRAHN-druh**

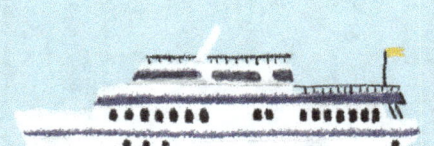

Boat ⇆ **Le bateau**
**luh bah-TOH**

Vehicles ⇆ **Les véhicules**
**lay vay-eh-KOOL**

Park ⇆ **Le parc**
**luh PARK**

Grocery store ⇆ **Le supermarché**
**luh soo-pair-mar-SHAY**

School ⇆ **L'école**
**lay-KOHL**

Hospital ⇆ **L'hôpital**
**loh-pih-TAL**

Train station ⇆ **La gare**
**lah GAR**

Library ⇆ **La bibliothèque**
**lah bee-blee-oh-TEK**

Cafe ⇆ **Le café**
luh kah-FAY

Restaurant ⇆ **Le restaurant**
luh res-toh-RAHN

Where do you like to go?
⇆ Où est-ce que tu aimes aller ?
oo ess kuh tew em ah-LAY

Town ⇆ **La ville**
lah VEEL

Pencil ⇆ **Le crayon**
**luh cray-YOHN**

Marker ⇆ **Le feutre**
**luh fuh-TRUH**

Crayon
⇆ **Le crayon de couleur**
**luh cray-YOHN duh koo-LUHR**

Book ⇆ **Le livre**
**luh LEEVR**

Paper ⇆ **Le papier**
**luh pah-PYAY**

Notebook ⇆ **Le cahier**
**luh kai-YAY**

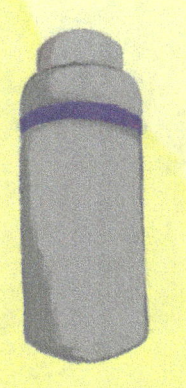

Water bottle ⇆ **La bouteille d'eau**
**lah boo-TAY doh**

Ball ⇆ **Le ballon**
**luh bah-LOHN**

Glue ⇆ **La colle**
**lah KOLL**

Eraser ⇆ **La gomme**
**lah GOM**

**What do you take to school?**
⇆ **Qu'est-ce que tu prends pour l'école ?**
**kes kuh tew prahn poor lay-KOHL**

Computer ⇆ **L'ordinateur**
**lor-dee-nah-TEUR**

School ⇆ **L'école**
**lay-KOHL**

Red ⇆ **Rouge**
ROO-j

Yellow ⇆ **Jaune**
JOHN

Blue ⇆ **Bleu**
BLUH

Green ⇆ **Vert**
VEHR

White ⇆ **Blanc**
BLAHN

Black ⇆ **Noir**
NWAHR

Brown ⇆ **Marron**
mah-ROHN

Purple ⇆ **Violet**
vee-oh-LEH

Pink ⇆ **Rose**
ROHZ

Orange ⇆ **Orange**
oh-RAHNJ

Gray ⇆ **Gris**
GREE

What's your favorite color?
⇆
Quelle est ta couleur préférée ?
kel eh tah koo-LUHR pray-fay-RAY

Colors ⇆ **Les couleurs**
lay koo-LUHR

1  2  3  4

One ⇆ **Un**
AHN

Two ⇆ **Deux**
DEUH

Three ⇆ **Trois**
TRWAH

Four ⇆ **Quatre**
KAH-tr

5  6  7  8

Five ⇆ **Cinq**
SAHN-k

Six ⇆ **Six**
SEES

Seven ⇆ **Sept**
SEHT

Eight ⇆ **Huit**
WEET

Can you count to ten?
⇆
Peux-tu compter jusqu'à dix ?
puh tew kon-TAY joos-kah DEES

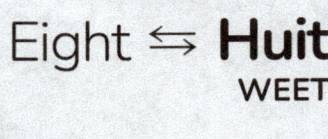

9  10

Nine ⇆ **Neuf**
NUF

Ten ⇆ **Dix**
DEES

Circle ⇆ **Le cercle**
**luh SEHR-kluh**

Square ⇆ **Le carré**
**luh kah-RAY**

Triangle ⇆ **Le triangle**
**luh tree-AHN-gluh**

Heart ⇆ **Le cœur**
**luh KUHR**

Crescent ⇆ **Le croissant**
**luh krwah-SAHN**

Arrow ⇆ **La flèche**
**lah FLESH**

Pentagon ⇆ **Le pentagone**
**luh pahn-ta-GOHN**

Rectangle ⇆ **Le rectangle**
**luh rek-TAHN-gluh**

Numbers & Shapes ⇆ **Les nombres et les formes**
**lay NOHN-bruh ay lay FORM**

Coffee ⇆ **Le café**
luh kah-FAY

Lavender
⇆ **La lavande**
lah lah-VAHND

Perfume
⇆ **Le parfum**
luh par-FUHN

Macaron
⇆ **Le macaron**
luh mah-kah-ROHN

Crepe ⇆ **La crêpe**
lah KREP

Mona Lisa
⇆ **La Joconde**
lah jo-KOHND

Carousel
⇆ **Le manège**
luh mah-NEJ

Croissant
⇆ **Le croissant**
luh krwah-SAHN

Baguette
⇆ **La baguette**
lah bah-GET

## Louvre Museum
⇆ **Le musée du Louvre**
luh myu-ZAY dew LOOVR

Eclair ⇆ **L'éclair**
lay-KLAIR

## Eiffel Tower
⇆ **La tour Eiffel**
lah toor eh-FELL

Chef ⇆ **Le chef**
luh SHEF

## Poodle
⇆ **Le caniche**
luh kah-NEESH

**What would you like to see?**
⇆ **Qu'aimerais-tu voir ?**
kem-ray tew vwar

Snail ⇆ **L'escargot**
less-kar-GOH

Things we love in France ⇆ **Ce qu'on aime en France**
suh kohn EM ahn FRAHNSS

Good evening ⇆ **Bonsoir**
**bohn-SWAHR**

Yes / No ⇆ **Oui / Non**
**WEE / NOHN**

Hugs and kisses ⇆ **Câlins et bisous**
**kah-LAN ay bee-ZOO**

Have a nice day
⇆ **Bonne journée**
**bohn-joor-NAY**

See you soon ⇆ **À bientôt**
**ah-byan-TOH**

Thank you for the meal
⇆ **Bon appétit**
bohn ah-peh-TEE

It was delicious
⇆ **C'était délicieux**
say-TAY day-lee-SYUR

**Help!** ⇆ **Au secours !**
oh skOOR

How are you?
⇆ **Ça va ?**
sah-VAH

I'm good
⇆ **Ça va**
sah-VAH

More useful phrases ⇆ **Phrases utiles**
FRAHZ yoo-TEEL

Toys ⇆ **Les jouets**
lay joo-EH

Doll ⇆ **La poupée**
lah poo-PAY

Robot ⇆ **Le robot**
luh roh-BOH

Gift ⇆ **Le cadeau**
luh kah-DOH

Donut ⇆ **Le beignet**
luh bay-NYAY

Juice ⇆ **Le jus**
luh JYU

Ice cream ⇆ **La glace**
lah GLASS

Cake ⇆ **Le gâteau**
luh gah-TOH

**What do you like the best?**
⇆ **Qu'est-ce que tu préfères ?**
kes kuh tew pray-FAIR

Chocolate ⇆ **Le chocolat**
luh shoh-koh-LAH

Things kids love ⇆ **Choses que les enfants aiment**
shohz kuh lay zahn-fahn EM

Amusement park ⇆ **Le parc d'attractions**
luh park dah-trak-SYOHN

Pool ⇆ **La piscine**
lah pee-SEEN

Birthday ⇆ **L'anniversaire**
lah-nee-vehr-SAIR

Swing ⇆ **La balançoire**
lah bah-lahn-SWAHR

Nap ⇆ **La sieste**
lah SYEST

Slide ⇆ **Le toboggan**
luh toh-boh-GAHN

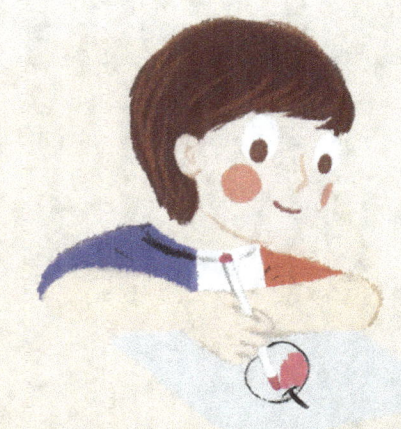

Maze ⇆ **Le labyrinthe**
luh lah-beer-AHNT

Coloring ⇆ **Le coloriage**
luh koh-loh-ree-AHJ

What do you think is fun?
⇆ Qu'est-ce que tu aimes faire pour t'amuser ?
kes kuh tew EM fair poor tah-mew-ZAY

Things kids love ⇆ **Choses que les enfants aiment**
shohz kuh lay zahn-fahn EM

Our trip to France is coming to an end...
But the adventure never ends.

Notre voyage en France touche à sa fin...
Mais l'aventure ne fait que commencer !

NOH-truh vwah-YAHJ ahn FRAHNSS toosh ah sah FAHN...
meh lah-von-TEWR nuh feh kuh koh-mahn-SAY

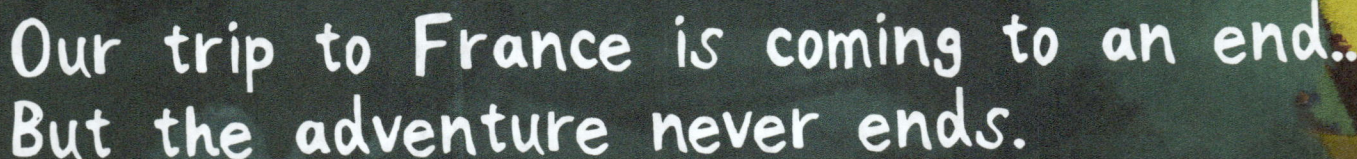

With every word you learn, your world can shine a little brighter.

À chaque mot que tu apprends, ton monde brille un peu plus.

ah shak moh kuh tew ah-PRAHN, ton mond BREE-yuh
uh puh plooss

Thank you for learning with me. Keep growing, keep smiling, and keep saying "Bonjour" to the world!

Merci d'avoir appris avec moi. Continue de grandir, de sourire, et de dire « Bonjour » au monde !

Mehr-SEE dah-VWAHR ah-PREE ah-VEK mwah kohn-tee-NEW duh grahn-DEER, duh soo-REER, ay duh DEER bohn-JOOR oh MOHND !

# The End
# La Fin

lah FAHN

# World Languages for Kids Series

The series introduces ten common words in 15 languages.

English, German, Russian, French, Spanish, Portuguese, Italian, Persian, Arabic, Hindi, Tagalog, Swahili, Mandarin Chinese, Japanese, and Korean

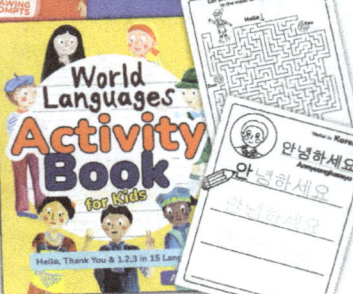

The 2nd series introduces ten common words in an additional 15 languages, including American Sign Language.

American Sign Language (ASL), Swedish, Dutch, Greek, Polish, Ukrainian, Hebrew, Amharic, Zulu, Tamil, Thai, Vietnamese, Indonesian, Cantonese, and Māori

Follow us on:

 FactorySachi (Instagram/Facebook/Pinterest)

Please visit our website to view more products!
FactorySachi.com